Wildflowers in Watercolour

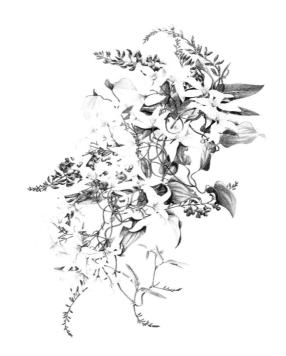

Dear Beryl,

Hope you enjoy this addition to your "Australia Collection"!

Love

Daphne & Ross

xxx

Wildflowers in Watercolour
– Journal –

Philippa Nikulinsky

FREMANTLE ARTS CENTRE PRESS

All nature is but art.
Alexander Pope

All art is but imitation of nature.
Lucius Annaeus Seneca

I first saw these elegant white flowers
cascading from trees on the banks
of the Oakover River, in the Pilbara.

Sesbania formosa (White Dragon Tree)

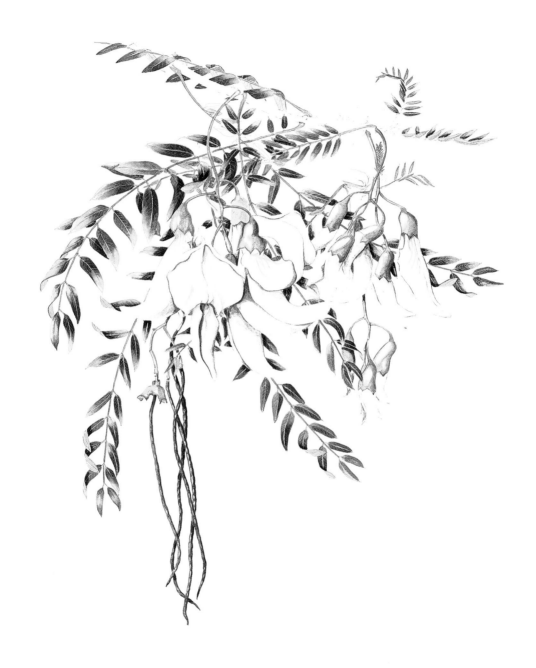

I look up in wonder at these
orchids growing on the trees in
the tropics.

Dendrobium canaliculatum (Antelope Orchid)

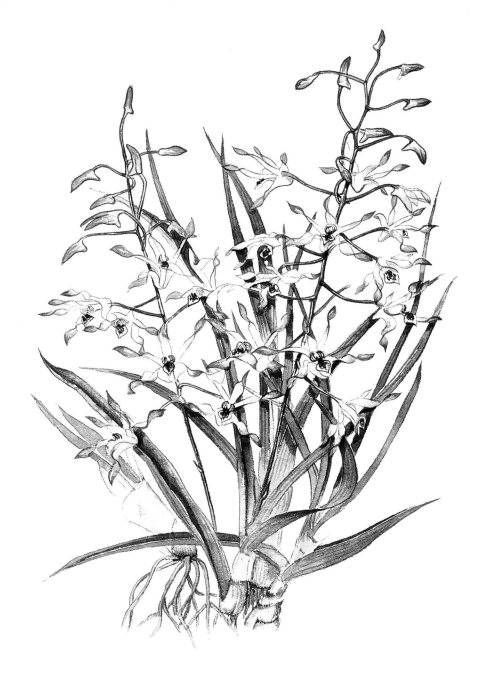

Late winter & early spring while everything still damp - just the Hardenbergia - then the clematis - tangling over each other, dripping with flowers.

Hardenbergia comptoniana (Native Wisteria) and
Clematis pubescens (Common Clematis)

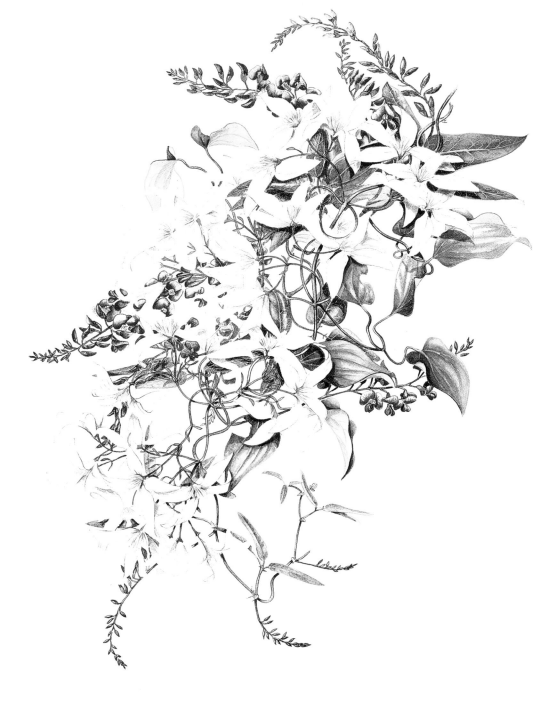

Lechenaultia, always irresistible.
Its beauty evokes a primordial ache
for all the ages of its existence.

Lechenaultia biloba (Blue Leschenaultia)

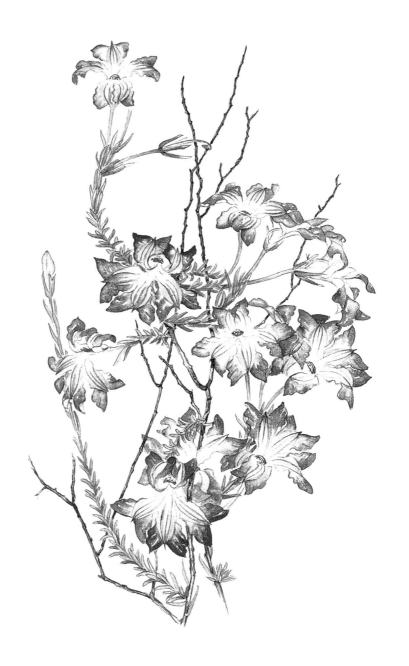

I sat on the river bank and just marvelled at their beauty.

Nymphaea violacea (Blue Waterlily)

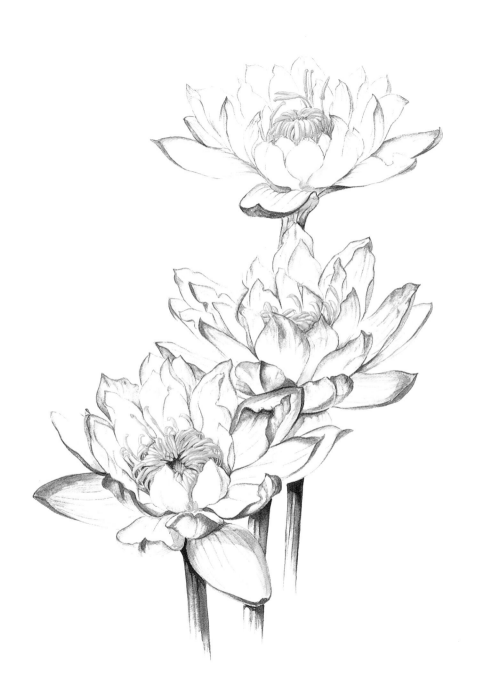

Recently someone called me an
"Eremophila freak". I agreed.
Eremophilas are irresistible. So
varied – Such a gentle beauty.

Eremophila freelingii (Stony Poverty Bush) and
Eragrostis eriopoda (Woollybutt Grass)

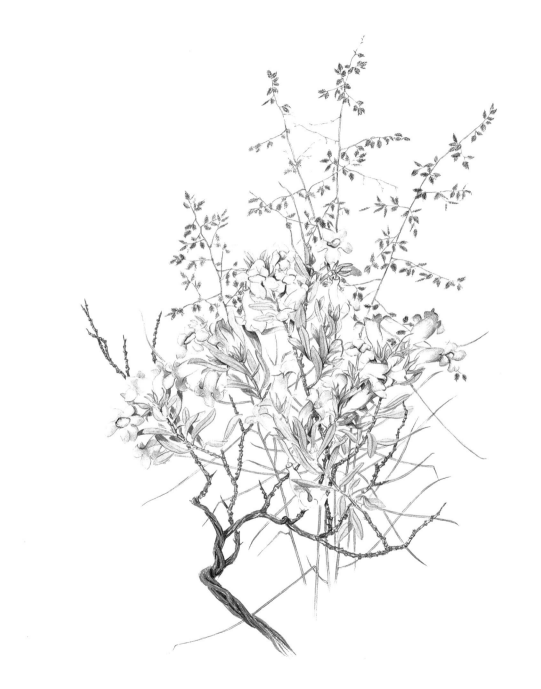

I followed a logger's track with huge karri & tinglewood trees meeting overhead and lichens, ferns and fungi underfoot on the spongy forest floor. Little gardens everywhere at my feet.

Gompholobium polymorphum (a climbing pea), *Dampiera hederacea* (Karri Dampiera), *Thelymitra crinita* (Blue Lady Orchid), *Lindsaea linearis* (Screw Fern)

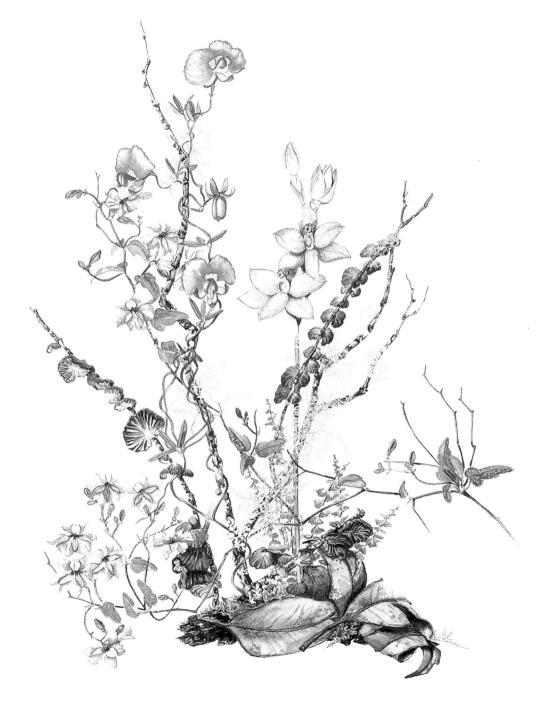

So many pink enamel orchids. Lovely
spots on back of buds & petals. Stypandra
miniature form. Are they just undeveloped
specimens of the usually tangled, spilling
stems from other rock gardens?
All the blues & pinks pretty together.
Watched the butterflies feeding on the
flowers. — seem similar to ones near
Balladonia, but no 'eye' spots.

Stypandra imbricata (Blind Grass), *Elythranthera emarginata* (Pink Enamel Orchid),
Pimelea species (a banjine) and *Andersonia lehmanniana* (a heath)

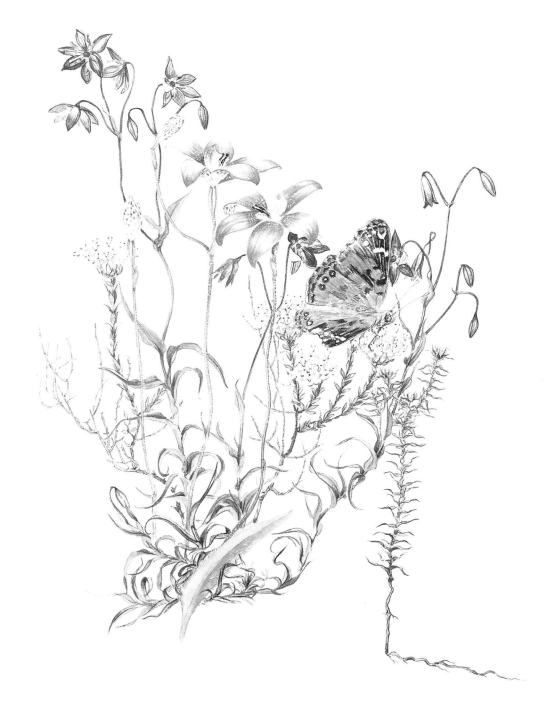

In the early morning the flowers
covered with icicles. The purple
flowers a beautiful contrast against
the grey smoke bush.

Calytrix eneabbensis (Eneabba Starflower)

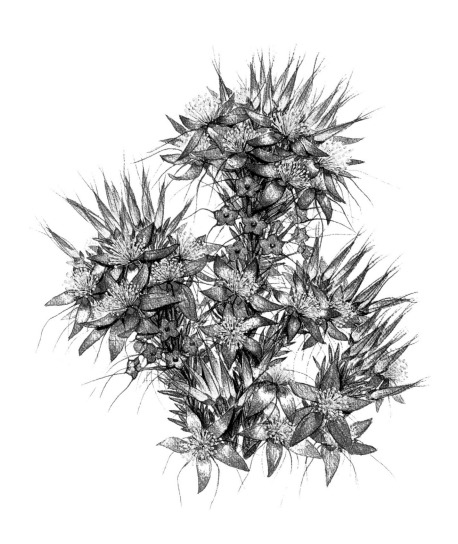

Again a tangled mass of orchids bouya & drosera. Many rock gardens no bigger than an old baby's bath. — each with its own predominant colour. In one the melding blues of the caladenia & blue lady orchids in another, the bright yellows of the sun orchid & sparkling orange of the drosera.

Drosera macrantha (Bridal Rainbow),
Thelymitra aff. *macrophylla* (a sun orchid) and *Cyanicula deformis* (Blue Fairy Orchid)

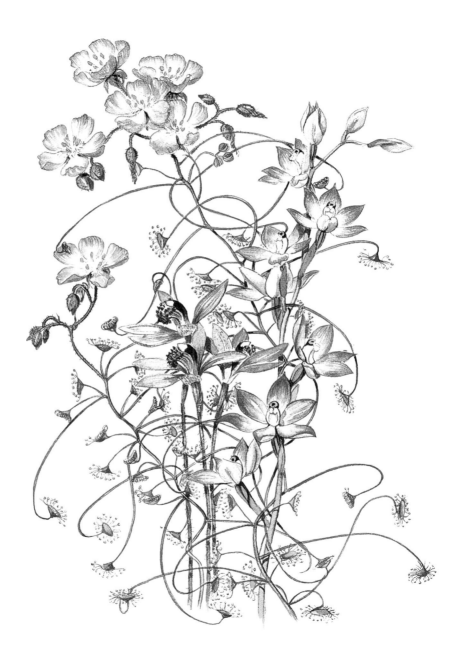

Blue sky, warm sun, biting cold wind. Winter in the desert, for me, is always eremophila.

Eremophila platycalyx (Granite Poverty Bush) and *Eremophila georgei* (a poverty bush)

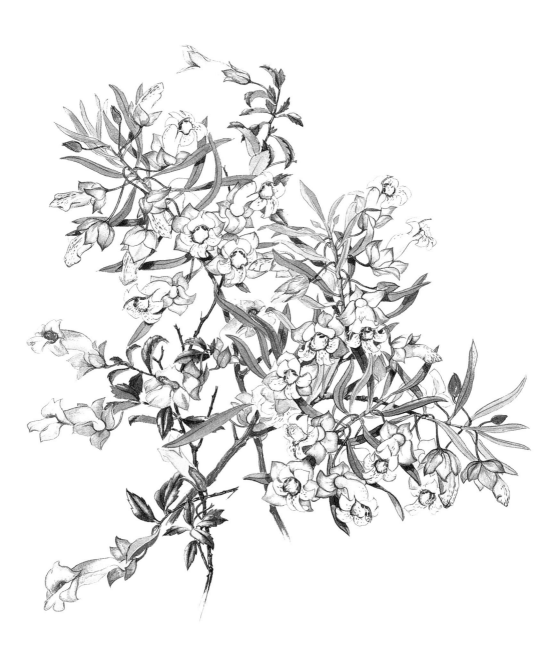

Beautiful mauve & pink of isotoma in massed displays with trigger plants in thousands at a lower story. all looked very pretty – no, beautiful!
Rocks in the forest not an exclusive sanctuary. Often I see the same plants away from the rocks. Everything softer – more delicate than inland drier outcrops where the contrasts are often startling

Stylidium calcaratum (Book Triggerplant), *Isotoma hypocrateriformis* (Woodbridge Poison) and *Laxmannia minor* (Paperlily)

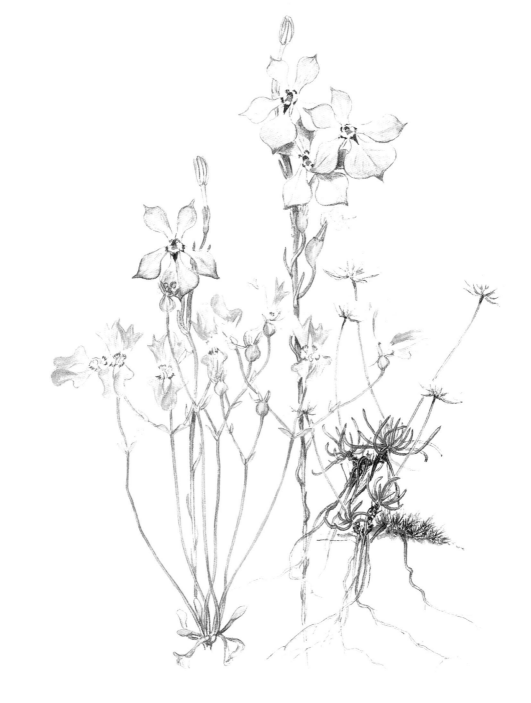

Found in a swampy area near a rainforest thicket on a friend's Kimberley cattle station. The longest 'eucalypt' leaves I'd ever seen.

Eucalyptus ptychocarpa (Spring Bloodwood)

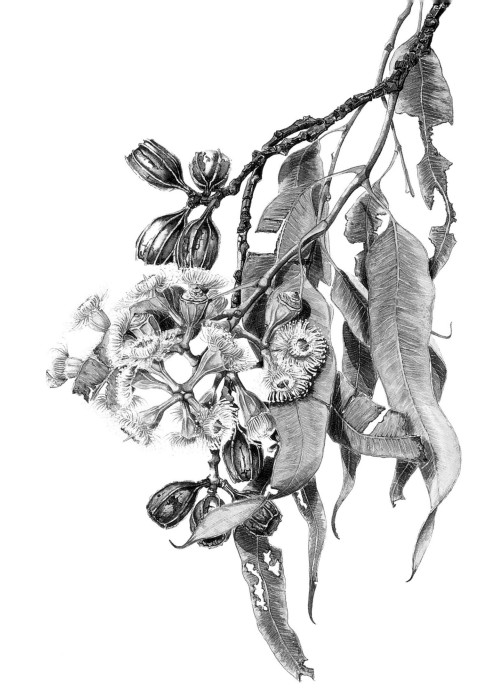

Bright green new leaves arrive with the flowers on the bare branches of this summer flowering tropical tree.

Brachychiton discolor (Kurrajong)

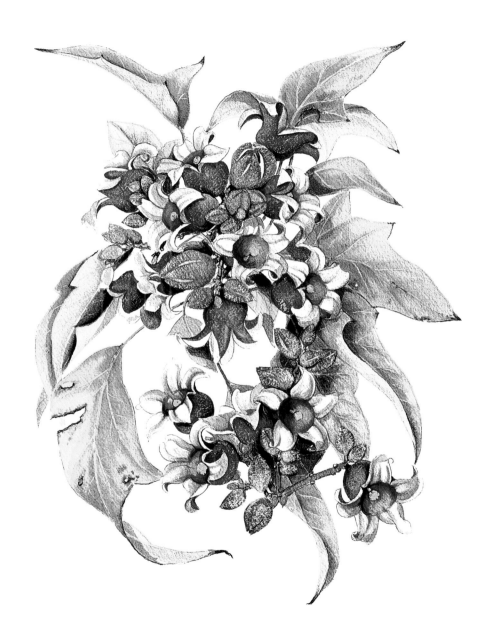

Always a very special flowering tree
My parents house was called Torquata.

Eucalyptus torquata (Coral Gum)

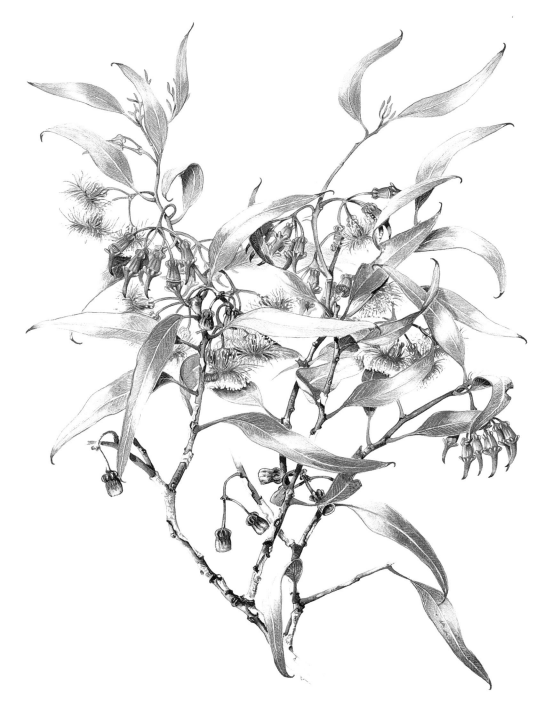

So common in gardens and
streets it is exciting to see these
rare, grand, old trees protected
in the rock hollows

Eucalyptus caesia subsp. *magna* (Silver Princess)

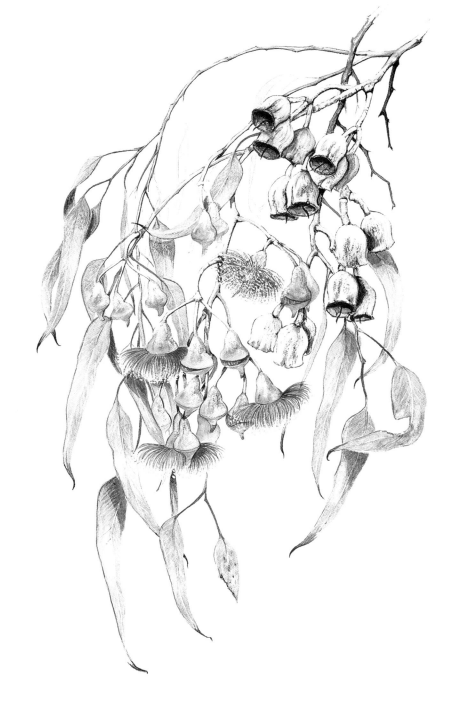

Growing together but aloof from each other on a granite outcrop in the goldfields.

Cymbopogon obtectus (Silkyheads) and *Drosera macrantha* (Bridal Rainbow)

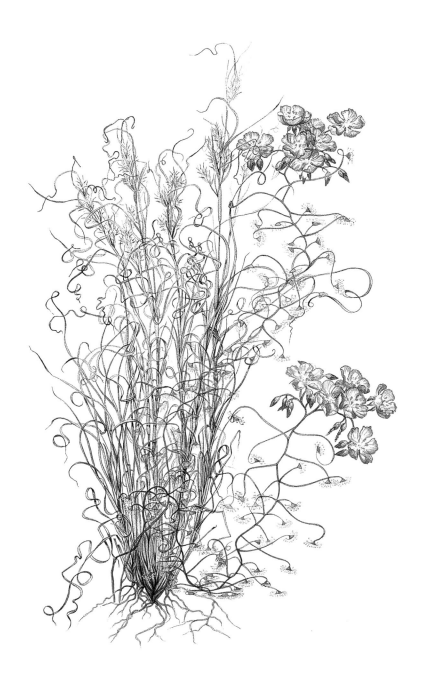

Proudly popping up through
the casuarina needles covering
the ground.

Caladenia sp. (Reaching Spider Orchid) and *Lindsaea linearis* (Screw Fern)

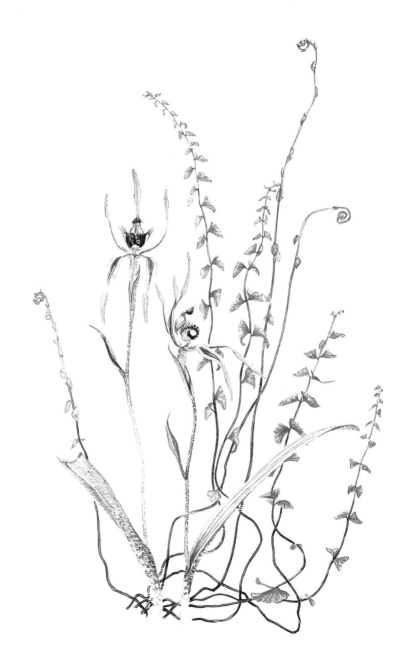

After the fire the regrowth is magic!

Tetratheca confertifolia (Kwongan Tetratheca) and
Isopogon divergens (Spreading Coneflower)

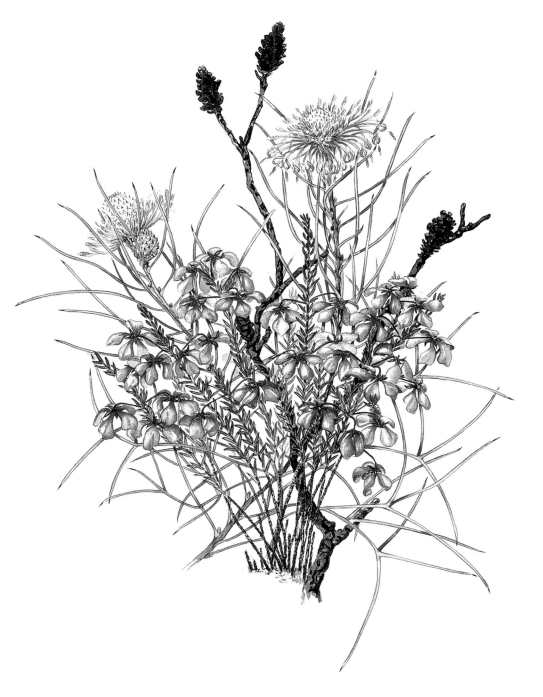

Mulgas scattered over the open
red loamy ground. Clumps of
spinafex sheltering the everlastings
which are always an indicator of
how good the wildflower season
will be.

Lawrencella davenportii (Sticky Everlasting) and
Eragrostis eriopoda (Woollybutt Grass)

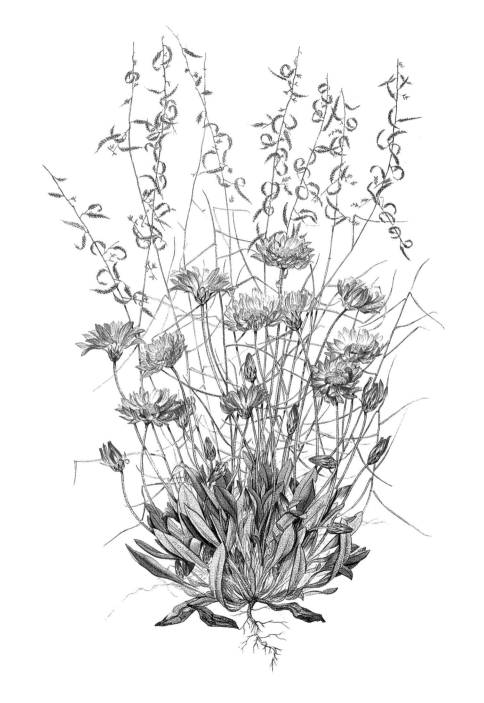

Its perfume led me to the boronia.
Not far away on the sand ridge
the isopogon. The flamboyant and
the inconspicuous.

Boronia megastigma (Scented Boronia) and *Isopogon formosus* (Rose Coneflower)

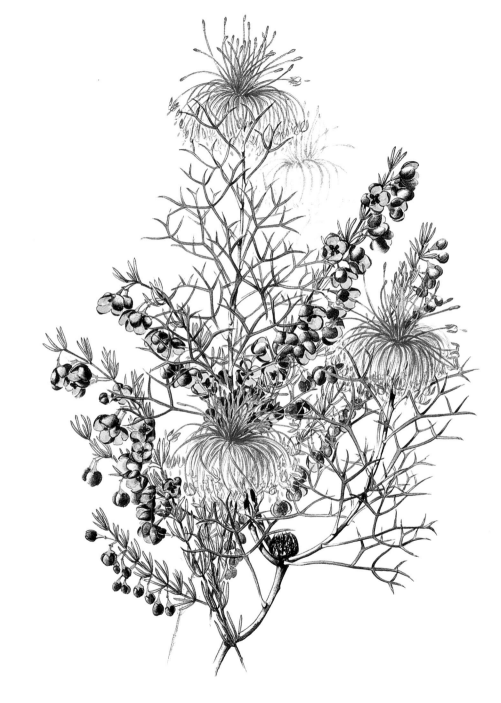

Walking in the forest, downhill towards a stream. — Far off laughter of children. An extravagance of flowers. Such peace and beauty so near the city.

Sowerbaea laxiflora (Purple Tassels), *Pterostylis recurva* (Jug Orchid),
Tetratheca hirsuta (Black Eyed Susan), *Acacia extensa* (Wiry Wattle),
Hovea chorizemifolia (Holly-leaved Hovea), *Anigozanthos humilis* (Catspaw),
Dryandra lindleyana subsp. *lindleyana* (Couch Honeypot),
Hybanthus calycinus (Wild Violet) and *Hibbertia lasiopus* (Large Hibbertia)

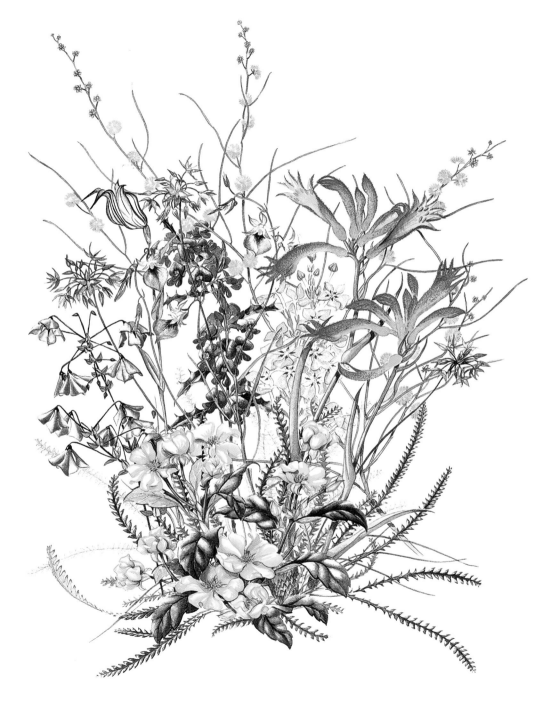

A soak at the end of a dusty track
flies everywhere - chains of yellow
everlastings in rippling waves
under the hissing cover of the
papery white splendida
Everlastings are childhood!

Rhodanthe chlorocephala subsp. *splendida* (Splendid Everlasting),
Cephalipterum drummondii (Pompom Head), *Rhodanthe* species (an everlasting) and
Ptilotus species (a mulla mulla)

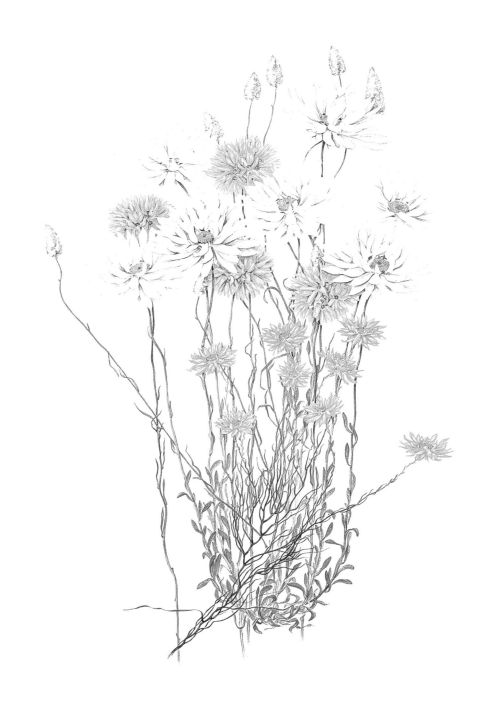

Soft grey leaves and yellow flowers
in scattered clumps over the
white sandplain.

Conostylis candicans (Grey Cottonhead)

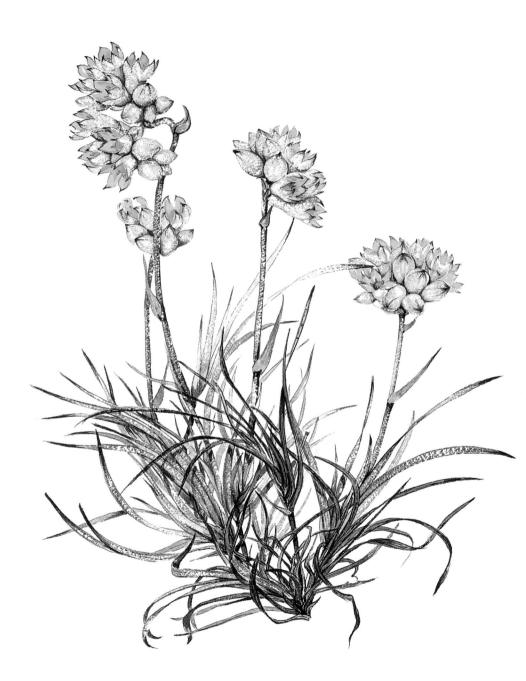

I haven't seen this growing in the wild, but a friend loved the tree in her front garden so I painted hers.

Hymenosporum flavum (Native Frangipani)

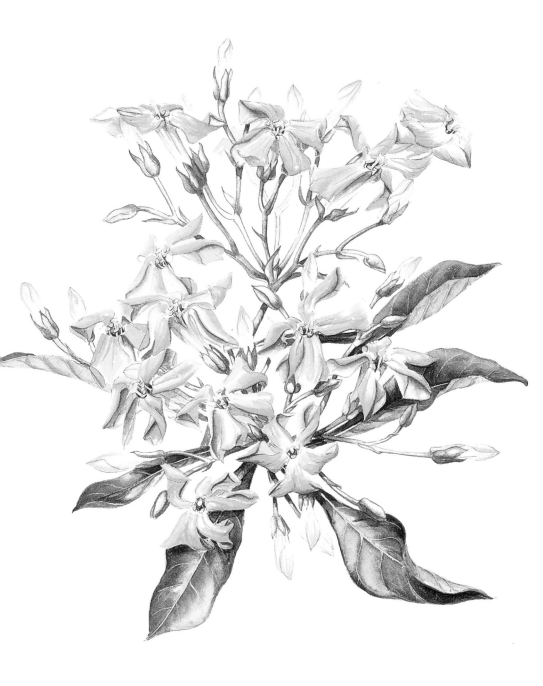

I spend days just sitting and watching the antics of little wren colonies.

Malurus assimilis (Purple-backed Wren) and *Acacia tetragonophylla* (Kurara)

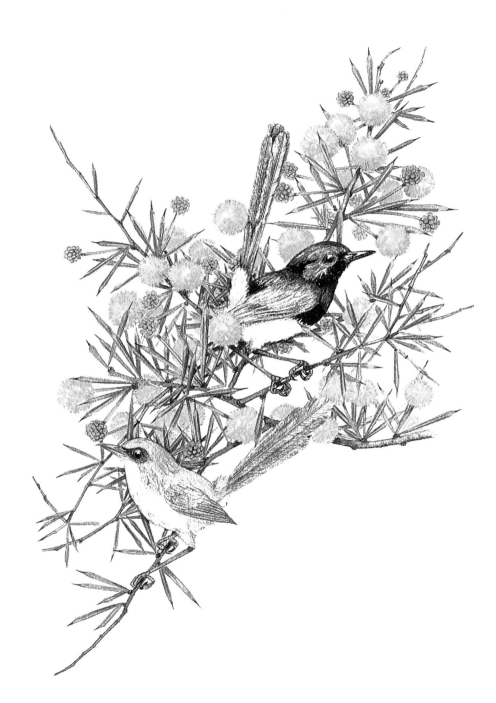

Pungent perfume and the ground
covered with fuzzy bright yellow.

Acacia tumida (Pindan Wattle)

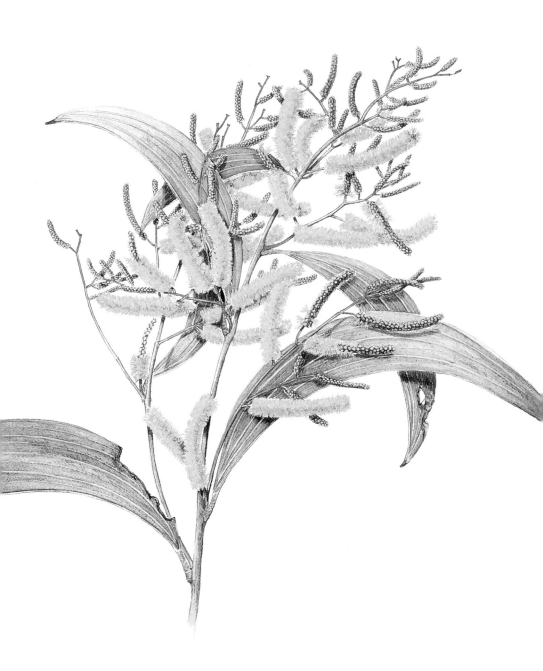

I found these orchids near black wet rocks in early spring when the forest was still dark and moody.

Diuris corymbosa (Common Donkey Orchid),
Pterostylis recurva (Jug Orchid) and *Pterostylis barbata* (Bird Orchid)

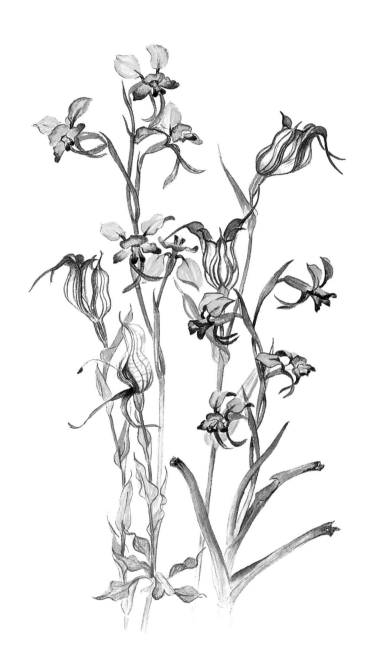

At the edge of the rock on the wet
peaty black soil — a leopard orchid.
Pterostylis nearly finished - most leaves
eaten off. Thelymitra starting to swell
with seeds.
Each "dancing to the music of time".

Thelymitra flexuosa (Twisted Sun Orchid), *Thelymitra benthamiana* (Leopard
Orchid), *Pterostylis* aff. *plumosa* (Bird Orchid) and *Borya nitida* (Pincushion)

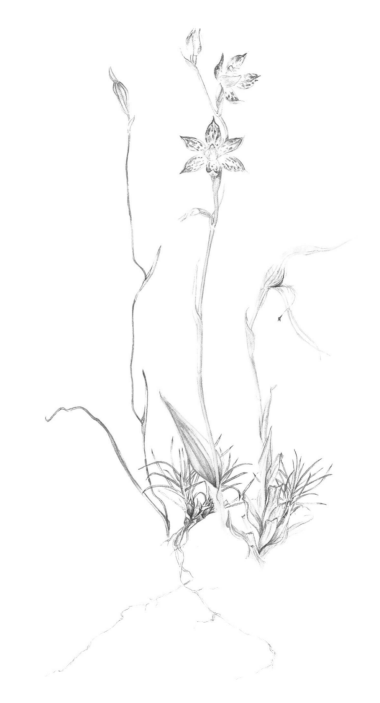

Scattered across the red desert sand,
The scraggly trees bent over with
the weight of the huge flowers and
old gum-nuts

Eucalyptus kingsmillii (Kingsmill's Mallee)

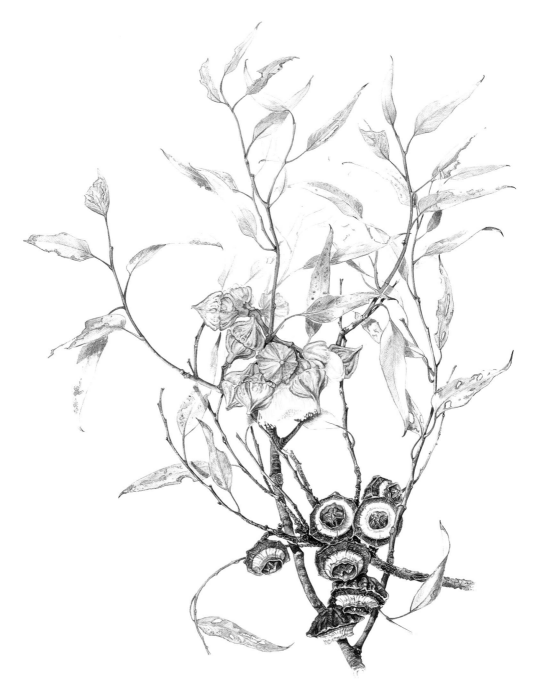

Unusually large, bright green phyllodes for
' Life on the Rocks'.
Massed on the rock apron in deeper soil
pockets.
Bright green and bright yellow – happy!
Flowers many on long stems
Not a lot of insect damage
Little hook on end of each phyllodes

Acacia lasiocalyx (Wilyurwur)

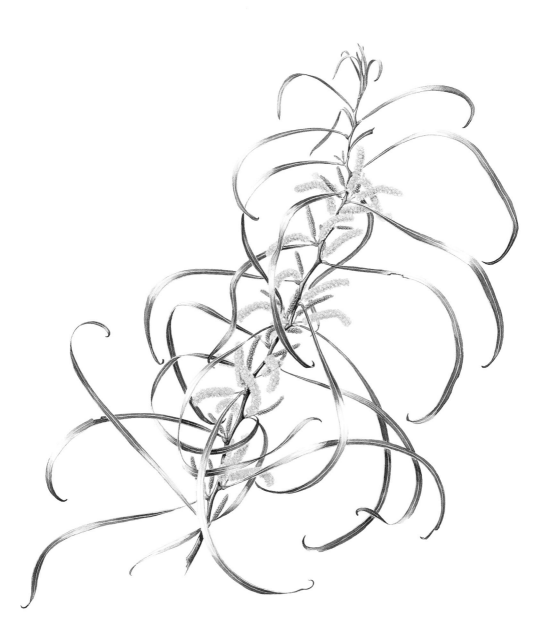

Golden candles in early summer.
The curling old fruiting cone reminds
me of 'Snugglepot & Cuddlepot'.

Banksia attenuata (Slender Banksia)

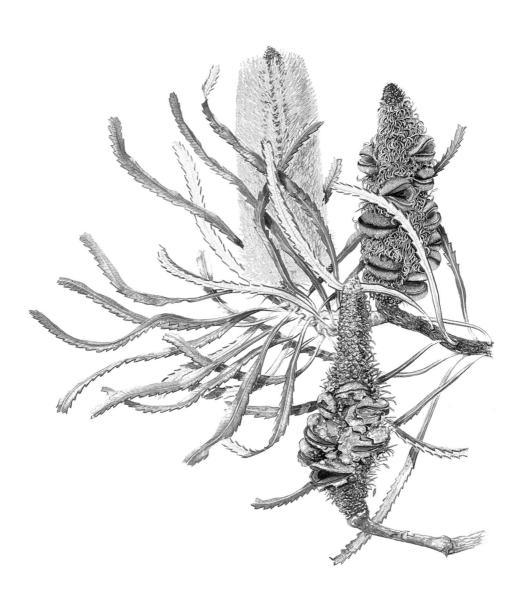

Golden filigree patterns spilling
over the rocks and under the trees.

Chamaexeros macrantha (Fringe-leaf Lily)

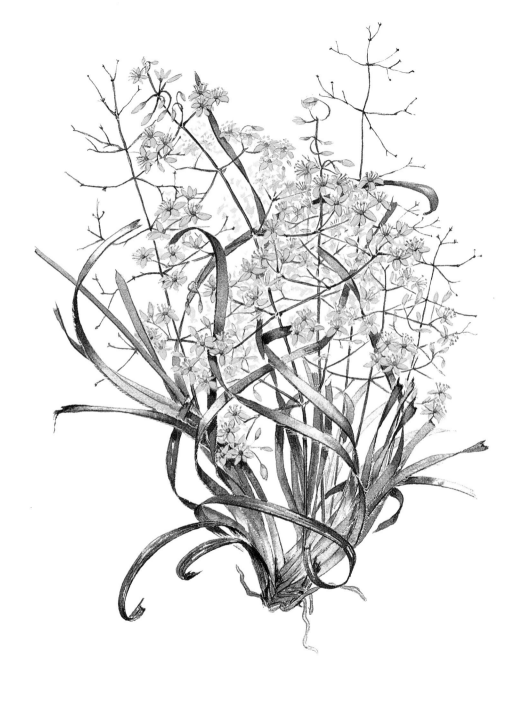

Gracefully spreading branches
drooping with the weight of the
flowers. — low hum of the bees.

Acacia baileyana (Cootamundra Wattle)

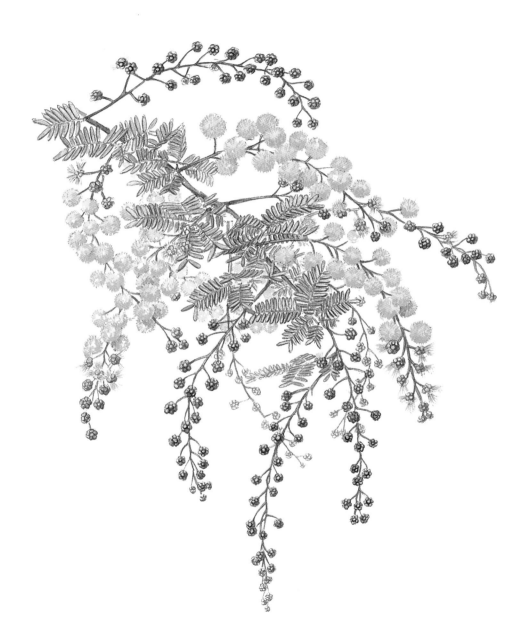

Sun bursts of flowers on bare
branches constrasting with the elegant
twists and curls of last year flower
stems.

Cochlospermum fraseri (Kapok Bush)

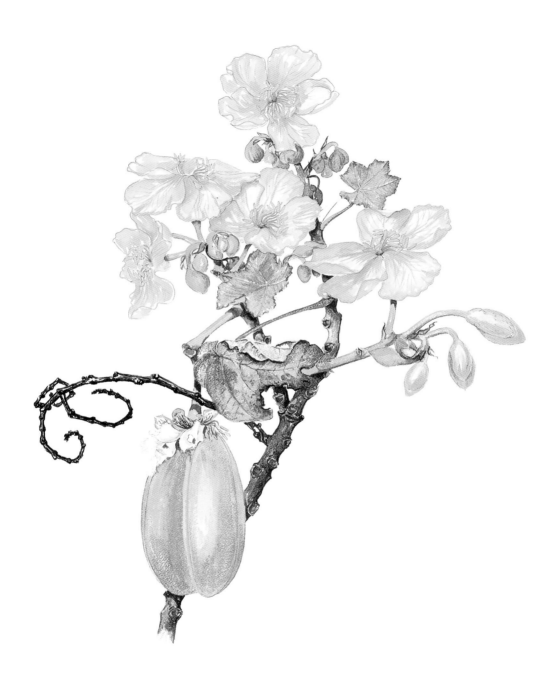

I've seen this eucalypt so often
in parks and gardens that there
is a sense of unreality seeing
it flowering in the bush.

Eucalyptus erythrocorys (Illyarrie)

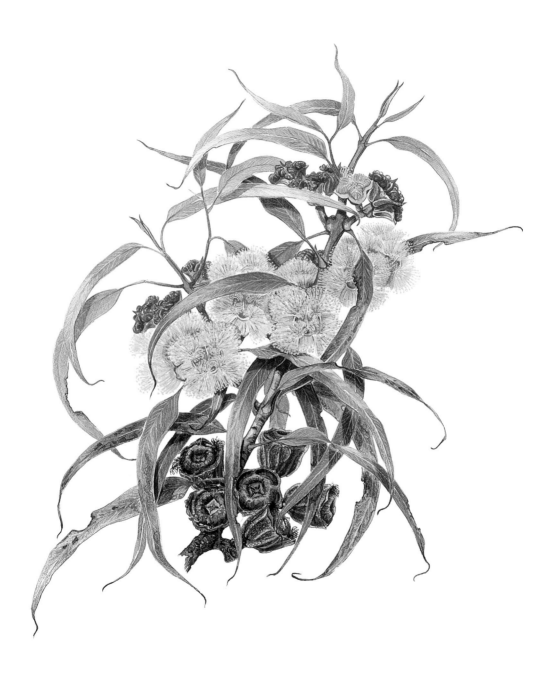

Cockroach bush - so well named.
Seed pods more interesting than
the flowers. A happy combination
of colours.

Senna venusta (Cassia), *Senna notabilis* (Cockroach Bush) and
Ptilotus schwartzii (a mulla mulla)

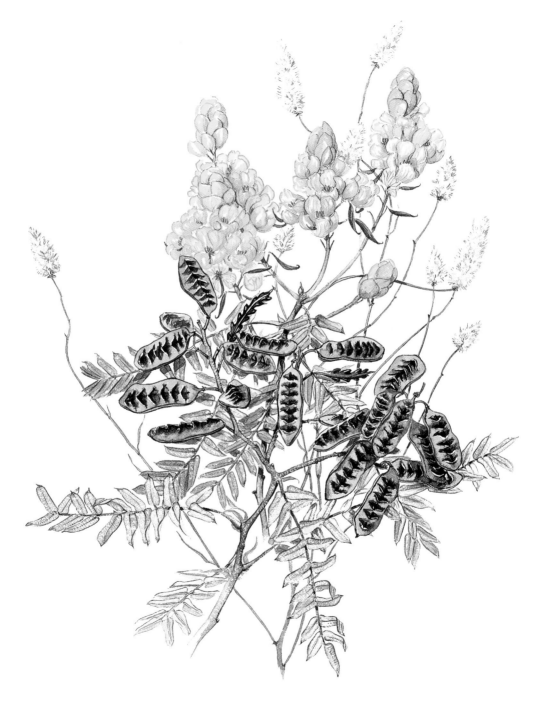

Dry, rough, tangled. A strange beauty revealed by familiarity.

Dryandra formosa (Showy Dryandra)

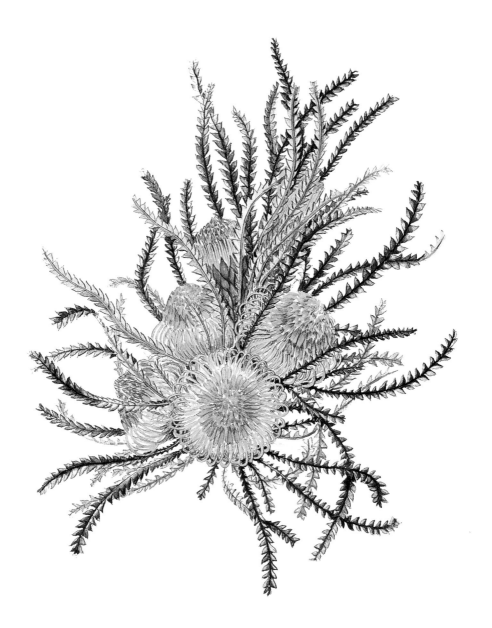

A desert field trip would not
be complete without the nectar-
rich eriostachya flowers swaying
on long stems in the wind.

Grevillea eriostachya (Orange Grevillea)

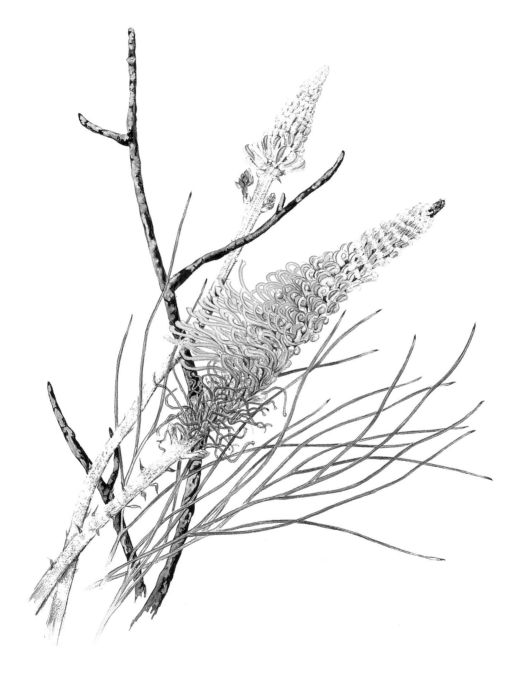

Enormous, tall, straight trunks. The ground covered with flowers nipped off by the parrots. My friend picked me a flowering branch out of their helicopter.

Eucalyptus miniata (Woollybutt)

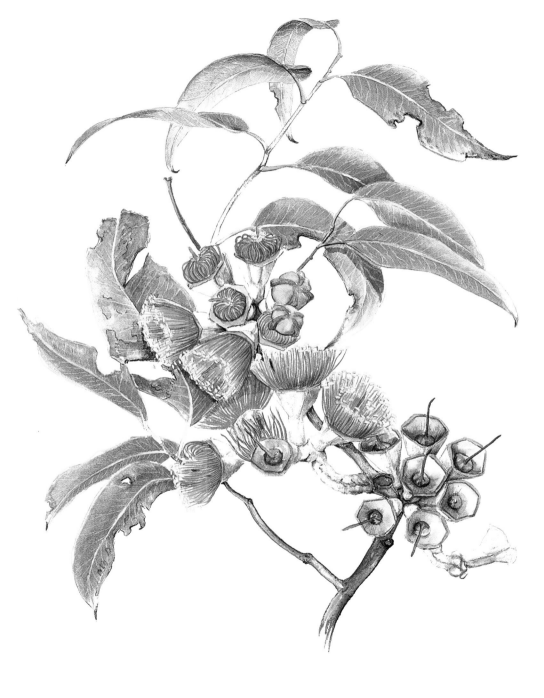

Coming upon bush pomegranites is
like finding a Japanese garden.
Small bushes like miniature trees,
gnarled & twisted, hung with
orange lanterns.

Balaustion microphyllum (Bush Pomegranate)

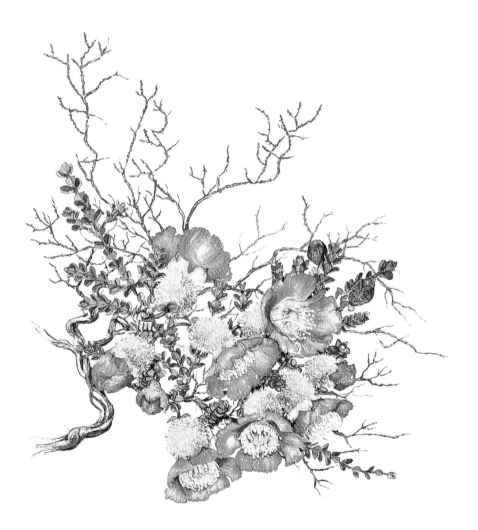

Hot and humid under the trees.
Out of the dark trunks and branches
sprout these bursts of colour.

Castanospermum australe (Black Bean Tree)

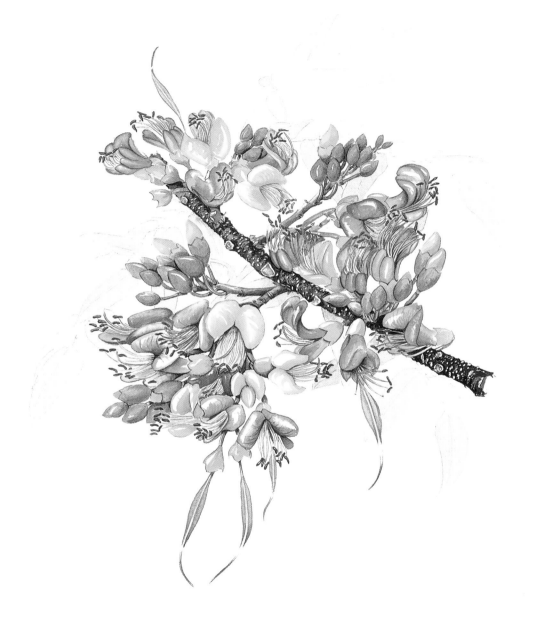

So visible on the white sandplain.
Every clump with different variation
of red and yellow flowers.

Lechenaultia formosa (Red Leschenaultia)

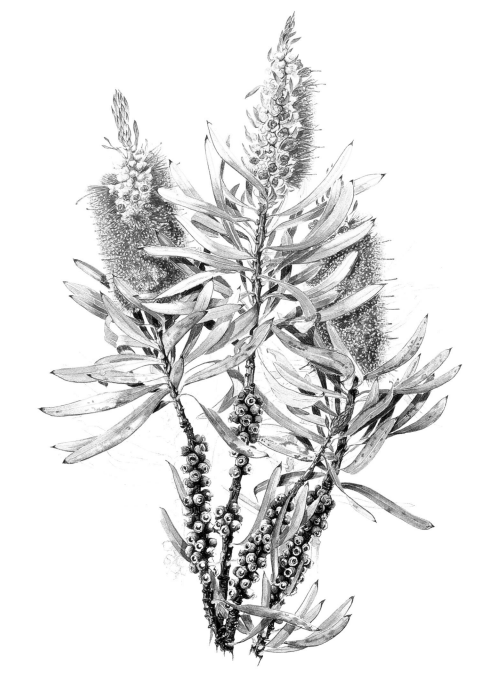

Vine exuberantly tangling over shrubs on ocean facing rocks. Covered with bright red flowers and reddy brown seed pods. I fell carrying all my drawing gear climbing on the slippery black rocks.

Kennedia beckxiana (Cape Arid Kennedia)

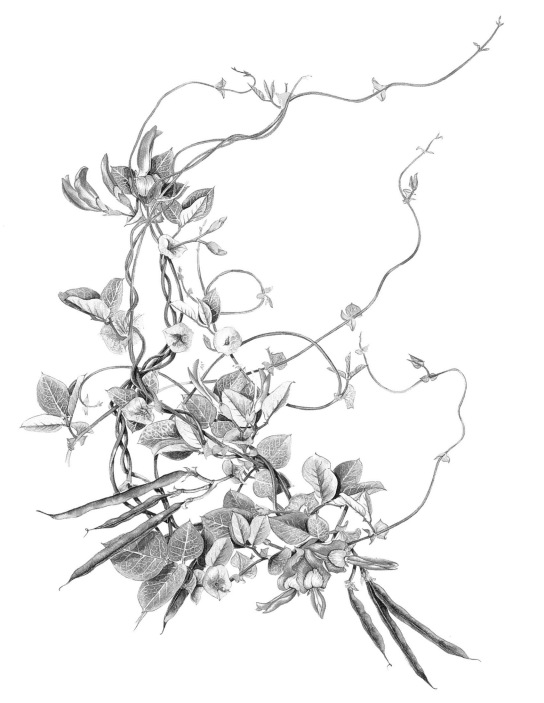

After rain, the usually scraggy shrubs are transformed – covered in red or cream clusters.

Kunzea pulchella (Granite Kunzea)

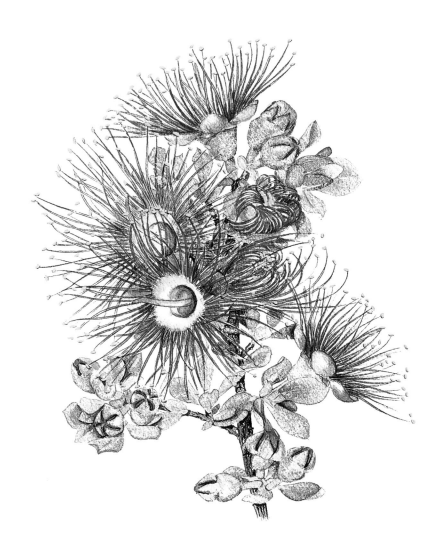

Dieback is now common where
these beautiful banksias were
once abundant.

Banksia coccinea (Scarlet Banksia)

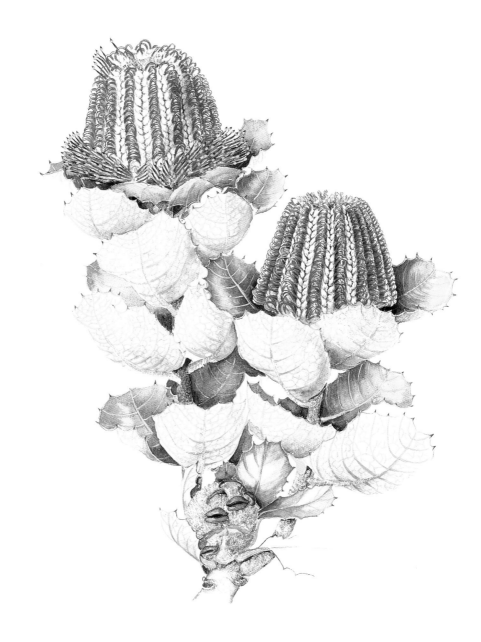

Dry, bare, rust red earth. Then after
the rain, as far as I can see,
sprawling, exuberant carpets of
red and green

Willdampia formosa (Sturt Pea)

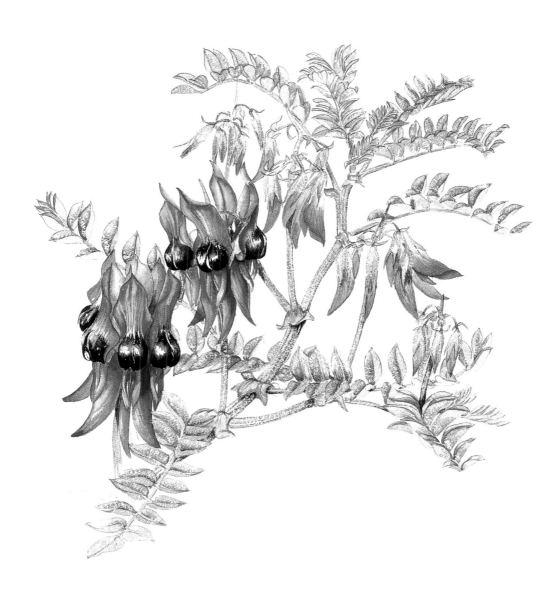

Flowering at the edge of a dry salt lake. The earth cracked and red. The flowers and grass look so delicate but are really tough survivors.

Eremophila maculata (Native Fuchsia),
Eremophila miniata (Kopi Poverty Bush) and *Eragrostis* species (a lovegrass)

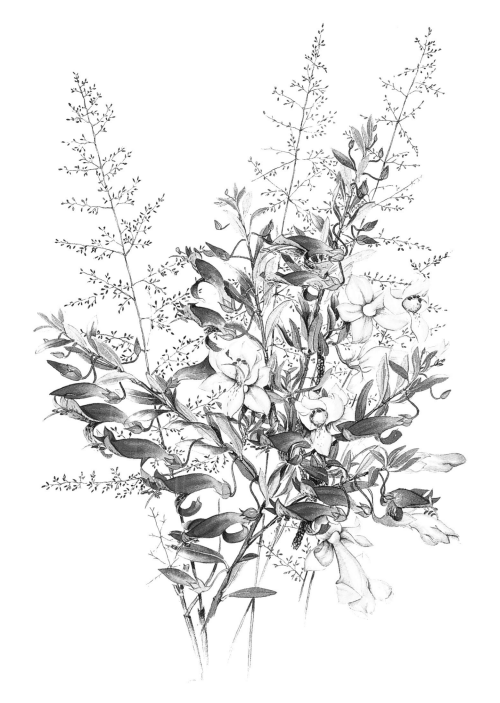

Only after the bushfire do the
verticordias look so grand with
the vitality and energy of the
"climactic flowering."

Verticordia grandis (Scarlet Featherflower)

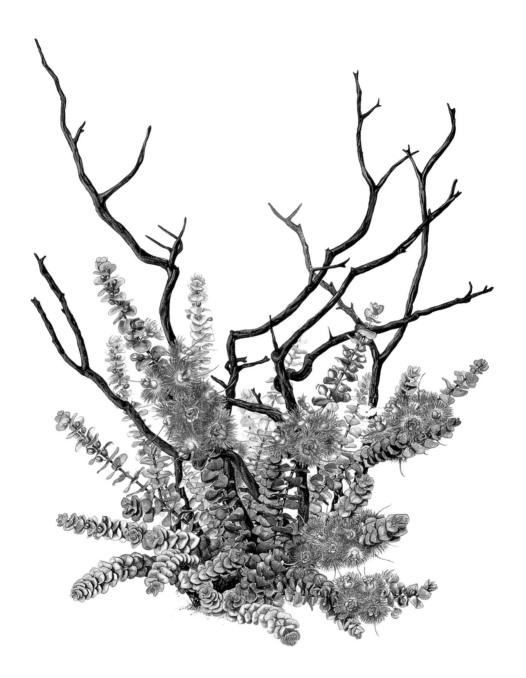

Quintessentially West Australian, these
kangaroo paws were not growing together
but painted to show their amazing
shapes and colours.

Anigozanthos manglesii (Mangles' Kangaroo Paw), *Anigozanthos pulcherrimus*
(Yellow Kangaroo Paw), *Anigozanthos rufus* (Red Kangaroo Paw),
Anigozanthos bicolor (Little Kangaroo Paw), *Anigozanthos humilis* (Catspaw) and
Macropidia fuliginosa (Black Kangaroo Paw)

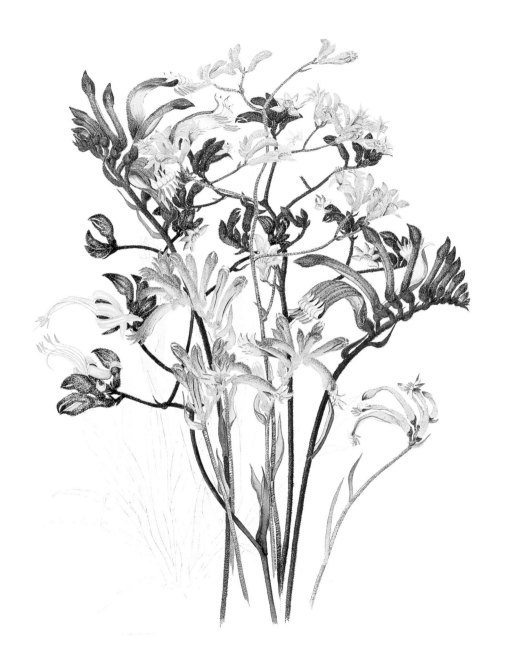

First published 2000 by
FREMANTLE ARTS CENTRE PRESS
25 Quarry Street, Fremantle
(PO Box 158, North Fremantle 6159)
Western Australia.
www.facp.iinet.net.au

Consultant Editor Alex George.
Production Coordinator Cate Sutherland.
Typeset by Fremantle Arts Centre Press.
Printed by South Wind Productions, Singapore.

The State of Western Australia has made an investment in this project
through ArtsWA in association with the Lotteries Commission.

Philippa Nikulinsky was born in Kalgoorlie, Western Australia, in 1942. She trained as an art teacher and has taught in a number of secondary schools and tertiary institutions. She now works full-time as a natural history artist and illustrator, specialising in Australian native flora.

Philippa's work has appeared in numerous group and solo exhibitions throughout Australia, and she has received many major public and corporate commissions in Australia and overseas. She has previously published four books — Western Australian Wildflowers in Watercolour, Banksia Menziesii, Life on the Rocks *(all published by Fremantle Arts Centre Press) and* Flowering Plants of the Eastern Goldfields of Western Australia. *She has also published seven illustrated diaries.*

Wildflowers in Watercolour

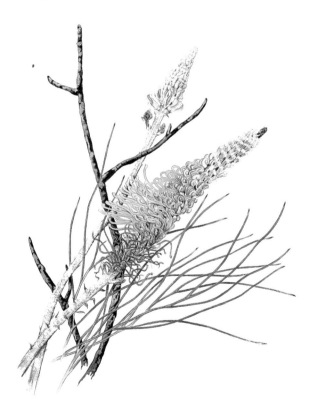